The Spirit of Deception

Byron K. Parker

The Spirit of Deception

Rediscovering True Light in a Dark Day

Foreword by

Dr. Bishop Vincent Mathews Jr, PH. D

The Spirit of Deception

Rediscovering True Light in a Dark Day

ISBN: 979-8-89704-586-0

Book Cover Design by Grant Partners Gospel

Published by:
Byron K. Parker Ministries
elderbyronparker@aol.com

Printed in the United States of America

Dedicated to the loving memory of my late mother, Myrtle Faye Parker Nesbitt. Who laid the foundation of prayer and the study of God's word, which has greatly enriched my life.

"Refresh your commitment today to test everything by the Word of God. The surest defense against spiritual deception is the knowledge of spiritual truth." Dr. David Jeremiah

Acknowledgment

A task of this magnitude could never be done alone. I am acutely aware of the love, prayers, and support of many special people who partnered with me to make this volume possible.

First and foremost, I want to thank God, from whom all blessings and knowledge flow. It is He who works within us, giving us both the will and the ability to fulfill His good purpose. Never in a million years would I ever think that I would write a book.

I thank my late mother, Myrtle Faye Parker Nesbitt, who was the most influential person in my life. This book is dedicated to her memory. For the God I serve was her God, the Bible that I read was her Bible, and the life I now live is the life she taught me to live.

To my brother, friend, and confidant, Derrick Grant, who has partnered with me in my ministry endeavors and has been a great encourager. He is the owner and solopreneur of Grant Partners Gospel and the Book Cover designer. Special thanks to his wife, Tracy, who provided this manuscript's proofreading, editing, and grammar correction (Friends are a gift from God).

To my mentor, Bishop, and friend, Bishop Anthony E. Harris Sr., Thank you for always being there and providing guidance along the way.

To my sister, Dr. Gena Ross, a brilliant author who has published six books. Thank you for providing the necessary framework on the business side to make this possible. You are an inspiration.

To a long-time, special sister, friend, and partner in ministry, Dr. Tichina Williams. Because of you, many ministry doors have opened for me. I entrusted you with a preview copy of this work. Thank you for your spiritual collegiate insight and professionalism.

I would also like to thank my prayer partners, *"The Weekend Warriors,"* who have prayed for me and with me for the last four years at 7:00 am every Saturday. Especially Sis. Linda Thomas, who spoke it saying, *"Elder Parker, you have the knowledge to write a book."*

To my siblings Napolean, Stephanie, Christopher, and Evelyn, they are the only ones who know my story like none other. I'm sure they're shocked, to say the least. Thank you for your love and support.

To the many saints who saw my political views and spoke into my life, many of them are now sleeping. Their words of instruction have proved valuable.

Last but certainly not least, I want to thank Bishop Vincent Mathews Jr., whom I asked at the last minute if he would write the foreword to this book. For many years, I have watched his standard of excellence while making an impact in the kingdom of God. He possesses the fortitude to stand in many areas of global influence. My admiration and respect are best stated in the scriptures that say, *"Mark the perfect man and behold the upright: for the end of that man is peace"* (Psalm 37:37).

Table of Contents

Foreword

In a world where deception and misinformation can spread like wildfire, it's more crucial than ever to discern truth from error. For years, Pastor Byron K. Parker has been passionate about warning believers about the dangers of deception, preaching, and teaching on this vital topic across the country. In *"The Spirit of Deception,"* he shares the culmination of his research and revelation from God. I have worked with him for many years and know he has a passion for God's people. This relevant and powerful book is proof positive.

Hosea 4:6 warns us that our *"People are destroyed for lack of knowledge."* Thus, this book is a timely and urgent call to the church to awaken to the reality of deception and its destructive power. With meticulous biblical analysis and prophetic insight, Pastor Parker exposes the enemy's tactics and equips readers to recognize and resist the spirit of deception.

As we navigate the complexities of our modern world, we need the discernment and wisdom that only comes from a deep understanding of God's Word. Pastor Parker's work is vital for believers seeking to safeguard themselves against the spirit of error and deception.

In the following pages, you'll discover the origin of deception, the importance of knowing God's word, and the power of knowledge in resisting deception. You'll also explore the vessels of deception, the doctrine of the air, and the great spiritual reversion. Each chapter carefully examines the biblical text applied to our contemporary context.

As you read *"The Spirit of Deception,"* I encourage you to approach the material with an open heart and mind, ready to receive the revelation and insight that God has given Pastor Parker. May this book be a catalyst for spiritual awakening and a deeper understanding of God's Word.

May we, as the Body of Christ, rise up with renewed vigilance and discernment, equipped to navigate the challenges of our times and to shine the light of truth in a world increasingly shrouded in deception.

With gratitude for Pastor Parker's obedience to God's call, I commend *"The Spirit of Deception"* to you, dear reader. May God bless you as you read and apply these vital truths.

Dr. Bishop Vincent Mathews Jr, PH.D

Pastor, Tabernacle Southaven COGIC Southaven, MS

INTRODUCTION

The Spirit of Deception

We have often heard that the day would come when we would not be able to tell the difference between right and wrong. The Bible makes it very clear that it would be a day of great deception in the last days. If it were possible, they would deceive the very elect. Consequently, we must safeguard ourselves against the spirit of error-deception. The lack of knowledge is the method that satan uses to employ deception, but God is never left without a witness whose discernment has been sharpened by the written Word of God. God has chosen his people on this dark day to shine the light on the spirit of deception so that we may rediscover true light. For this is a day of knowledge, and the hidden things are being revealed.

As the final battle intensifies, we cannot emerge in deception. We must fully know the spirit of error and the spirit of truth so that we may be able to *"Comprehend with all saints what is the breadth, and length and depth, and height and to the love of Christ, which passed knowledge, that ye might be filled with all the fullness of God"* (Ephesians

3:18-19).

To the believer, our spiritual comprehension is through the Word of God. Therefore, we must understand the importance of God's Word in our lives. Let us remember what the Lord said to us through the words he spoke to Joshua.

This book of the law shall not depart out of your mouth: but thou shalt meditate therein day and night, that thou mayest observe to do according to all that is written therein: for then thou shalt make your way prosperous and then thou shalt have good success. (Joshua 1:8)

The Psalmist says that the man who meditates day and night "Shall be like a tree planted by the rivers of water that bring forth his fruit in his season. His leaf also shall not wither, and whatsoever he doeth shall prosper" (Psalm 1: 2-3). These scriptures tell us that if one meditates day and night and obeys the word of the Lord perpetually, he will prosper in life. For God holds a special place in His word. We see that He exalts His word above His name.

The Bible says that "Heaven and Earth would pass away but my word shall not pass away" (St. Matthews 24:35). And, "When he could swear by no greater, he swears unto himself that he would keep his word" (Hebrews 6:16). We see that God is very protective over His word. The Bible tells us that "God watches over his word, and he would hasten to perform it" (Jeremiah 1:12). It further tells us, "The word of the Lord is a light unto our pathway and lamp unto our feet" (Psalm 119:05).

As we study The Spirit of Deception, let us do so by the word of the Lord.

CHAPTER 1

The Origin of Deception

"The fundamental deception of satan is the lie that obedience can never bring happiness." R.C. Sproul

The Dispensation of Innocence

From the beginning of time, we see the human race has been prey to the spirit of deception. This spirit had its inception in the Garden of Eden, in a time of innocence.

Now the serpent was more subtil than any beast of the field which the LORD God had made. And he said unto the woman, Yea, hath God said, Ye shall not eat of every tree of the garden? And the woman said unto the serpent, We may eat of the fruit of the trees of the garden: But of the fruit of the tree which is in the midst of the garden, God hath said, Ye shall not eat of it, neither shall ye touch it, lest ye die. And the serpent said unto the woman, Ye shall not surely die: For God doth know that in the day ye eat thereof, then your eyes shall be opened, and ye shall be as gods, knowing good and evil. (Genesis 3:1-5)

When we study the seven dispensations of man, we see that the first dispensation is called the *"Dispensation of Innocence."* This was the time from the creation of the human race until the fall of man in the Garden. God created man after his own likeness and image. He placed man in the Garden of Eden and provided for him all of the necessities of life.

God gave man dominion over the works of his hands, the beast of the earth, the fowls of the air, and the fish in the sea. He blessed man to rule over the earth. During this time, we see that God and man have fellowship. The Bible says that God would come down in the cool of the day and commune with man.

He saw that it was not good for man to be alone and blessed man with companionship, and man called her woman. Man is commanded to be fruitful, multiply, and replenish the earth. However, God placed restrictions on man in relation to what he could and could not do. God commanded man that *"Of every tree of the garden, you may eat freely, but of the tree of knowledge of good and evil, thou should not eat of it, for the day you eat thereof thou shall surely die."*

The human race was content and in perfect harmony with God, until one day, all this changed through the spirit of deception. According to the Bible, satan approached the woman in the form of a cunning serpent, asking a seemingly simple yet deceptive question: *"Hath God said?"* This question planted doubt, a tactic satan used to mislead. His nature is one of deception, seeking to rob humanity of its divine connection. The Bible tells us that *"Satan comes to kill, steal and destroy"* (St. John 10:10).

Know Your Enemy

When we study the characteristics of a person, we see who they really are and what they are all about. It is said that a person's name reveals their true nature. When we study the names of satan, we get a better glimpse of who he is. One of the greatest strategies of warfare is to know your enemy. The primary mission of the United States military branches is to provide timely, tactical, and relevant intelligence in electronic warfare and tactic operation-level command.

Their mission is to always be prepared with appropriate intelligence to defend our liberties and come against our foreign and domestic enemies. Likewise, God the great Commander-in-Chief also provided us with the intelligence of his word, that we may be able to fight a good warfare and lay hold of eternal life.

Therefore, we must understand that one of satan's main weapons of mass destruction is deception. As we study the characteristics of satan by studying his name, we realize that deception is in his DNA. He is known by the following names:

- **The Father of Liars and Murderers:** *Ye are of your father the devil, and the lusts of your father ye will do. He was a murderer from the beginning, and abode not in the truth, because there is no truth in him. When he speaketh a lie, he speaketh of his own: for he is a liar, and the father of it. (St. John 8:44)*

- **Deceiver:** *"And the great dragon was cast out, that old serpent, called the Devil, and Satan, which deceiveth the whole world: he was cast out into the earth, and his angels were cast out with him." (Revelation 12:9)*
- **Thief:** *"The thief cometh not, but for to steal, and to kill, and to destroy: I am come that they might have life, and that they might have it more abundantly." (St. John 10:10)*
- **Adversary:** *"Be sober, be vigilant; because your adversary the devil, as a roaring lion, walketh about, seeking whom he may devour." (1 Peter 5:8)*
- **Accuser of the Brethren:** *"And I heard a loud voice saying in heaven, Now is come salvation, and strength, and the kingdom of our God, and the power of his Christ: for the accuser of our brethren is cast down, which accused them before our God day and night." (Revelation 12:10)*
- **False Angel of Light:** *"… for Satan himself is transformed into an angel of light." (2 Corinthians 11:14)*
- **The Prince of this World:** *"Now is the judgment of this world: now shall the prince of this world be cast out." (St. John 12:31)*
- **The God of this World System:** *"In whom the god of this world hath blinded the minds of them which believe not, lest the light of the glorious gospel of Christ, who is the image of God, should shine unto them." (2 Corinthians 4:4)*

When we see all of these things, we know that they are methods of deception.

The Love of the World

Satan deceived humanity in the Garden by using the love of the world. As the ruler of this world's system, he used the element of the world to misled the first Adam as he was created a living soul; to lose his inheritance through deception. Similarly, satan attempted to tempt the second Adam, Jesus, in the wilderness using the same tactics. However, unlike the first Adam, Jesus, was made a quickening spirit. Therefore, he overcame the enemy's schemes.

We are warned in the scripture to:

> *Love not the world, neither the things in the world. If any man loves the world, the love of the Father is not in him. For all that is in the world, the lust of the flesh and the lust of the eye and the pride of life is not of the Father but is of the world. (1 John 2:15-16)*

These same temptations were present in the Garden:

- **The Lust of the Flesh**: *"When the woman saw that the tree was good for food."*
- **The Lust of the Eye**: *"And that it was pleasant to the eye."*
- **The Pride of Life:** *"And the tree was to be desired to make one wise."*

The same way that satan deceived man in the Garden is the same way satan tried to deceive Jesus in the wilderness. The Bible says that God leads Jesus into the wilderness to be tempted by the devil. Since the beginning of time, man has always had to prove if he would love the "Lord thy God with all his heart, soul, and mind."

Jesus came into the world to fulfill all righteousness (St. Matthew 3:15), and He also had to go through a time of temptation and testing so that He would be our High Priest who could be touched by the feeling of our weakness and understand infirmities. *"Whereby we could come boldly to the throne of Grace to obtain mercy so He would be able to help us in time of need"* (Hebrews 4:15-16).

Jesus in the Wilderness

> *"And Jesus being full of the Holy Ghost returned from Jordan, and was led by the Spirit into the wilderness, being forty days tempted of the devil. And in those days he did eat nothing: and when they were ended, he afterward hungered." (St. Luke 4:1-2)*

During Jesus' time of testing and trial, the enemy resorts to an old, familiar tactic. Satan is limited in strategies, an old dog with old tricks. His power is limited, and he can only go as far as God allows, as seen in the testing of Job. Likewise, when tempting Jesus, satan uses the same three elements of the world that led to humanity's fall from grace.

- **The Lust of the Flesh:** *And the devil said unto him, 'If thou be the Son of God, command this stone that it be made bread.' And Jesus answered him, saying, 'It is written, that man shall not live* by *bread alone, but by every Word of God.' (St. Matthew 4:3-4)*
- **The Lust of the Eye**: *And the devil, taking him up into a high mountain, shewed unto him all the kingdoms of the world in a moment of time. And the devil said unto him, 'All this power will I give thee, and the glory of them: for that is delivered unto me; and to*

whomsoever I will I give it. If thou therefore wilt worship me, all shall be thine.' And Jesus answered and said unto him, 'Get thee behind me, Satan: for it is written, thou shalt worship the Lord thy God, and him only shalt thou serve.' (St. Matthew 4:8-10)

- • **The Pride of Life:** *And he brought him to Jerusalem, and set him on a pinnacle of the temple, and said unto him, 'If thou be the Son of God, cast thyself down from hence: For it is written, He shall give his angels charge over thee, to keep thee: And in their hands, they shall bear thee up, lest at any time thou dash thy foot against a stone.' And Jesus answering said unto him, 'It is said, Thou shalt not tempt the Lord thy God.' (St Matthew 4:5-7)*

In all of these instances, satan used the spirit of deception to cause Jesus to lose out on his spiritual inheritance with God. This reveals that satan is a master deceptor because he deceived himself and was expelled from heaven. Satan tried to ascend to the height of God and be like God. The Bible tells us that satan said the following:

- *"I will ascend into heaven."*
- *"I will exalt my throne above the stars of God."*
- *"I will sit also upon the mount of the congregation."*
- *"I will ascend above the height of the clouds."*
- *"I will be like the Most High." (Isaiah 14:14)*

It was the spirit of deception that hid the iniquity that was found in satan and caused him to become prey to his own devices. The Bible says that it is the god of this world system (satan) that blinds the mind of humanity so that they cannot see the glorious gospel of Jesus Christ. This will cause one to be unable to recognize their need to be saved and change, which is a life lived with unrest, without peace and bondage to sin.

Doubt

Satan came to the woman and said, *"You shall not surely die, For God knows that the day you eat of this fruit you shall be like gods knowing good and evil" (Genesis 3:4-5).* He caused her to believe that God was withholding something good from her. He played on her innocent emotion to cause her to want something she always had. The Bible says that *"God has given us all things that pertain to life and godliness"* (2 Peter 1:3)

"And whatever state we find ourselves in to be content" (Philippians 4:11). The enemy will often make us think that what we have is not enough to sustain life. This is a lie because we can make it even on broken pieces. (Acts 27:44) When we doubt the Word of God, we open ourselves to the spirit of deception and begin to sink into the ocean of life. Even as Peter kept his eyes on Jesus (who is the Word of God), he was able to safely navigate through the winds, waves, and storms of life, but when he allowed the spirit of deception to take his eyes off of Jesus, he began to fail.

The Bible says, *"The light of our body is our eyes"* (St. Matthew 6:22). God further promised he would guide us with his eyes (Psalm 32:8). We have often heard our eyes are the gateway to our soul. The soul refers to temporary things around us and our feelings, emotions, and passions. We must understand that the things we see are temporary and are often controlled by the god of this world system. The things we do not see are eternal.

If we are not careful, the spirit of deception, which is the enemy himself, will cause us to concentrate on the wrong things, which causes us to miss the mark and sin against God. While satan employed the spirit of deception in the Garden and the wilderness with man and Jesus, this is the same device he uses on us today. He subtly twists God's Word to cause us not to believe what God said. He wants us to think that there is more to life than what God has to offer. This is the original purpose of satan, and he does this by employing the spirit of deception.

CHAPTER 2

The Command to Know

"The more you know, the more you grow." Byron K. Parker

The New Testament writer John the Apostle gives an eyewitness account of the life and ministry of Jesus Christ. Although some have questioned his authorship, most scholars believe this is the same John who walked with Jesus.

Beloved, believe not every spirit, but try the spirits whether they are of God: because many false prophets are gone out into the world. . Hereby know ye the Spirit of God: Every spirit that confesseth that Jesus Christ is come in the flesh is of God. And every spirit that confesseth not that Jesus Christ is come in the flesh is not of God: and this is that spirit of antichrist, whereof ye have heard that it should come; and even now

> *already is it in the world.6. We are of God: he that knoweth God heareth us; he that is not of God heareth not us. Hereby know we the spirit of truth, and the spirit of error. (1 John 4:1-3.6)*

At the time of this writing, it is said that John, known as the *"Elder"* or *"Elder Statesman,"* is the only living original of the 12 disciples. The others had been martyred for their belief in Christ. He writes to us as a father to little children, providing instructions to be aware of trickery, scams, and falsehoods.

Many years after the death and ascension of our Lord and Savior Jesus Christ. There now arose a second, third, and fourth generation of believers, a time marked with a great deal of heresies and false teachings. After the great move of the church age, the word of the Lord grew mighty, and many believed in the name of Jesus Christ, confessing him as their savior. Those who opposed the faith began to avert the truth and taught contrary doctrines, which caused great confusion in the body of Christ. Many claimed to be true apostles but denied that Jesus Christ, the promised Messiah, had come in the flesh. John saw the need to write a pastoral epistle to the churches at large to warn, instruct, and advise them regarding the original teachings of Jesus Christ.

> *"Beloved, believe not every spirit, but try the spirits whether they are of God: because many false prophets are gone out into the world." (1 John 4:1)*

> *"Beware of false prophets, which come to you in sheep's clothing, but inwardly they are ravening wolves. Ye shall know them by their fruits. Do men gather grapes of thorns, or figs of thistles? So, every good tree bears good fruit, but the bad tree bears bad fruit." (St. Matthew 7:15-17)*

The Synoptic Gospels record Jesus' primary teaching called the *"Sermon on the Mount,"* its entirety is found in the book of Matthew. In the days of Jesus' ministry, he takes his new converts and gives them foundational teachings that shape their lives forever. This is what I call the fundamental principles of righteous living. It is often said that the best is saved for last; people may not remember everything you have said, but they are most likely to remember the first and last words spoken.

Beware of False Prophets

In the Mount Olive Discourse, Jesus warns his followers to be aware of false prophets. The followers asked what the signs were of the end of the world. The first words Jesus spoke. *"Take heed that no man deceives you"* (St. Matthew 24:4).

Jesus knew that the time would arise that great deception would be on the earth, and many would speak things in direct opposition to his teachings. He counteracts this by warning them about things to come.

He teaches that some will not have real relations with the truth. Jesus called them false prophets. A prophet speaks as a mouthpiece for God by divine inspiration or the preached word. The word false denotes error, untrue, or delusory. It is something that is not in accordance with truth or facts. It is incorrect. It may appear real, but in reality, it's fictional.

Therefore, Jesus is saying to his disciples to be aware of untrue mouthpieces. He further explains to his followers that they would be in sheep's clothing, but on the inside, they would be ravening wolves. The Bible says, *"That men look on the outward appearance, but God looks at the heart"* (1 Samuel 16:7). *"Keep thy heart with all diligence; for out of it are the issues of life"* (Proverbs 4:23).

As believers, we are sheep (or flock). Jesus is known as the Great Shepherd, who leads us into all spiritual truths and who will lay down his life for his sheep. One of the characteristics of a sheep is the need to be fed. Sheep require daily meals to maintain a healthy life. Sheep are often social eaters; this can run the risk of eating food that is not good for their digestive system. Sheep are farm animals that run in packs. They, for the most part, have the same outward appearance, and it is hard to tell them apart. This is why a false sheep can come among the flock and pretend to be real, but Jesus in his teaching to his followers gives us distinct descriptions to know the false from the real. Sheep do not lead sheep. *"For he said my sheep knows my voice, but a stranger will not follow."* (St. John 10:5,27) Sheep speak as the Shepheard speaks.

Jesus, being the High Priest of our faith and profession, set the example in his relationship with God. We hear Jesus saying that,

> *"I and My Father are one." (St. John 10:30)*
>
> *"For I have not spoken of myself; but the Father which sent me, he gave me a commandment, what I should say, and what I should speak." (St. John 12:49)*

"But that the world may know that I love the Father; and as the Father gave me commandment, even so I do. Arise, let us go hence." (St. John 14:31)

Real sheep are never independent of the Shepherd (Father). They do as they see him, follow where he goes, and only say what he says. John's guidance stems directly from Jesus' original teachings, emphasizing the importance of knowing and faithfully following them.

In the banking industry, there is a department dedicated to preventing currency and fraudulent transactions. It is called the Fraud Department. In this area, there are trained specialists dedicated to recognizing suspicious activities. Their training is spent understanding what is real from what is false. They study the real as it is always used as their barometer in identifying the false. As we study the Word of God, we move forward. This will sharpen our sense of knowing the spirit of error and the spirit of truth. The Word of God is always our barometer for recognizing the false from the real.

CHAPTER 3

The Umpire of Our Soul

"The presence of the Holy Spirit is the keystone of all our hopes."
John Nelson Darby

John the Elder tells his readers to *"know the Spirt of God."* If we are going to survive in a hostile post-ascension age, we must be diligent in knowing the Spirit of God. These were Jesus' final instruction to his followers before his crucifixion and departure in the clouds to be seated on His Father's right hand. Here, John again inserts the original teaching of Jesus into his words to the new generation of believers. He tells them that which was imparted unto him by Jesus Christ the Savior himself.

> *"But ye have an unction from the Holy One, and ye know all things." (1 John 2:20)*
>
> *Hereby know ye the Spirit of God: Every spirit that confesseth that Jesus Christ is come in the flesh is of God: And every spirit that confesseth not that Jesus Christ is come in the flesh is not of God: and this is that spirit of antichrist, whereof ye have heard that it should come; and even now already is it in the world. (1 John 4:2-3)*
>
> *And I will pray the Father, and he shall give you another Comforter, that he may abide with you for ever; Even the Spirit of truth; whom the world cannot receive, because it seeth him not, neither knoweth him: but ye know him; for he dwelleth with you, and shall be in you. I will not leave you comfortless: I will come to you. Yet a little while, and the world seeth me no more; but ye see me: because I live, ye shall live also. (St. John 14:16-19)*

- The word comforter in Greek and Latin is as denoted as *Paraclete*
- In the gospel, the word Paraclete is translated into English as *Comforter*
- However, In the Epistle, it is translated as an *Advocate*
- Which actually means the same things: *Advocate or Helper*

It is said that the greatest thing a parent can leave to their children is not what they give them but rather what they leave in them. The old saying is that if you give a man a fish, you have fed him one meal, but if you teach him how to fish, you have fed him for a lifetime. The New Testament writer, John, sets a very interesting departing story before us. Jesus takes his 12 disciples, whom he had chosen to walk close with him in his earthly ministry. It is a defining moment because he speaks to them again about departing from them.

The disciples had some complexities with the fact that Jesus would no longer be their leader. He spent time teaching them in the high and low places. They had seen the mighty act of his ministry.

- He was their teacher; they were present when he taught them the Sermon on the Mount.
- They were present when he taught them the value of being a fisher of men.
- They were present when he taught them what is known as the Mount Olive Discourse.
- They were with him in good times.
- They learned how to stand with him even in times of controversy.
- They saw him feed the multitude.
- They witnessed the miracles of healing and deliverance.
- He provided guidance through rough times and words of encouragement, rebuke, and corrections.

Jesus' departing words carried the weight of a farewell, much like the final words of a loved one. In the spring of 2018, my mother pulled me aside and told me, *"Let me go. I am ready to go home to be with the Lord."* In that moment, I understood what the disciples must have felt. Though Jesus had previously told them he would not remain, the reality of his departure was deeply surreal.

To comfort them, Jesus began by saying, *"Let not your heart be troubled"* (St. John 14:1). He reassured them that His Father's house had many mansions and that he was going to prepare a place for them, promising to return and receive them. The disciples, seeking clarity, asked questions, eager to fully grasp what he was saying.

Thomas said, "... *We know not whither thou goest and how can we know the way?*" (St. John 14:5). Jesus responded, *"I am the way, the truth, and the life no man comes to the Father but by me"* (St. John 14:5). Similarly, Philip asked Jesus to show them the Father. Jesus gently reminded him, saying that after being with them for three and a half years, he had already revealed the Father through himself.

Jesus understood that the world his disciples would inherit after his departure would be one of great hostility. Throughout his ministry, controversy and opposition followed him. Even before his birth, there was turmoil—when Mary, betrothed to Joseph, was found to be with child by the Holy Spirit.

History also records that Herod the Great, nearing the end of his brutal reign, ruled through fear and violence. Upon hearing that the Messiah was to be born, He ordered the massacre of all infants in Bethlehem in a desperate attempt to eliminate the Savior.

The Scribes and the Pharisees often questioned his loyalty and observance of the Mosaic Law. He was questioned because he healed and worked miracles on the sabbath day. He was questioned because he entertained sinners.

Therefore, He prepared them to becomer fishers of men. He gave him the tools to survive in the world. Jesus says to them that it was necessary for you that *"If I do not depart from you the Comforter would not come"* (St. John 16:7). He further explains to the disciples that He whom the Father will send would dwell on the inside of them and would be with them always. Jesus had dwelt with them, but the Comforter would dwell in them.

He that the Father would send would be an *umpire to their soul.* In baseball, an umpire is the person charged with officiating the game, including the beginning and ending of the game. His job is to enforce the rules of the game and make judgment calls on plays. He would be the one who would alert them when something is not right. Likewise, the Holy Ghost is the umpire of our life with Christ. It is his job to alert us when something is amiss or not right.

He does this by placing an unction in our spirit. The Bible tells us that, *"But ye have unction from the Holy One and ye know all things" (1 John 2:20)*. An unction is a divine guidance that is manifested deep in the spirit of the believer. When the believer's spirit is made one with the Father. The Holy Spirit will be an umpire that provides knowledge and helps us to know the difference between error and truth. For the Holy Spirit is known as *"The Spirit of Truth."*

> *"Even the Spirit of truth; whom the world cannot receive, because it seeth him not, neither knoweth him: but ye know him; for he dwelleth with you, and shall be in you." (St. John 14:17)*

The above scripture says that the spirit of truth dwells on the inside. It is a defense mechanism against the spirit of deception and would lead you into all spiritual truths. The Holy Ghost on the inside would alert you when something is not right.

The Holy Spirit Will Testify of Jesus

John the Elder tells us that many will say that Jesus Christ has not come in the flesh and that they are still waiting on another Messiah. Many of the Jews thought that the Messiah would be a political ruler. They thought he would restore the kingdom of Israel back to the Jews. That he would be a conqueror and take the kingdom out of the hands of Herod. Herod also thought this. This was why he sought to destroy Jesus even from birth.

Jesus' primary purpose was to restore man back to God the Father. This was the opposite of what the Jews understood. As a result, many people denied that He was the true Messiah, as spoken by the prophets. As a result, the deity of Jesus was being questioned.

In the days of John the Elder, many were saying that Jesus Christ had not come in the flesh. In the life of Jesus Christ, many false prophets were saying that Jesus Christ was not the true Savior of the world. Even John the Baptist had a moment of doubt. When he was arrested and placed in prison, he sent his disciples to ask Jesus, *"Are you the one, or do we look for another?"* (St. Matthew 11:3). Throughout Jesus' earthly ministry, many of his followers went back and followed him no more. The Bible says, *"He came to his own, and they received him not"* (St John 1:11). In times of pressure, even Peter, who was in Jesus' inner circle, denied him thrice.

When Jesus had risen from the dead, Thomas said he would not believe it unless he saw the nail marks in Jesus' hands and put his finger where the nail print was. After Jesus makes himself known to

Thomas. Thomas exclaimed. *"My Lord and my God."* Jesus replied to him. *"You believe because you have seen, but blessed are those that have not seen but yet believe"* (St. John 20:28-29).

This is the reason why Jesus tells his followers that it is essential that you receive the Holy Ghost because: *"He would testify that I have come in the flesh and the blessings of believing would be yours."* The spirit of the antichrist denies that he has come in the flesh; this is a spirit of deception that works in the world to cause men to miss the blessing of believing.

> *"We are of God: he that knoweth God heareth us; he that is not of God heareth not us." (1 John 4:6)*

Jesus taught His followers that, "The words that I speak unto you they are spirit, and they are life." He also says:

> *Therefore, whosoever heareth these sayings of mine, and doeth them, I will liken him unto a wise man, which built his house upon a rock: And the rain descended, and the floods came, and the winds blew, and beat upon that house; and it fell not: for it was founded upon a rock. And everyone that heareth these sayings of mine, and doeth them not, shall be likened unto a foolish man, which built his house upon the sand: And the rain descended, and the floods came, and the winds blew, and beat upon that house; and it fell: and great was the fall of it. (St. Matthew 7:24-27).*

Jesus said I am the rock and stone which symbolizes a sure foundation. He knew that having the Holy Spirit inside of the believer would be very beneficial to them, and it would always cause them to believe that Jesus Christ was the son of God.

The early days that John followed Jesus, he came to Him on one particular occasion and said, *"Master, we saw one casting out devils in your name, but he followed us not, and we forbade him."* Jesus tells John that if they are not against us, they are a part of us. (St. Mark 9:38-40) Jesus taught his followers to know the spirit of error and the spirit of truth. Those who walk contrary to the teaching, doctrines, and principles, without precept and example, have been deceived by the spirit of error. Those who follow these teachings and the example of Jesus Christ and His words live in the spirit of truth.

Jesus knew that the spirit of deception would be at an all-time high as the times and laws would change to create falsehoods that cause men not to know the difference between right and wrong. So, he offered them a solution: the person of the Holy Ghost. The empire of our souls is the spirit of truth. He will be our helper on the inside, alerting us when truth is not present.

CHAPTER 4

The Doctrine of the Air

"All the cunning of the devil is an exercise trying to tear us away from the word." Martin Luther

In a previous chapter, we learned that satan is the prince of the power of the air. Having ruled this space, he has a legal right to employ false doctrines and teachings. When something floats in the air, it has a wide range that can affect many. This is the operation of the spirit of deception that satan uses for mankind to buy into his lies to deceive. For us to fully understand this, we must dig deeper into the word of the Lord.

"Wherein in time past ye walked according to the course of this world, according to the prince of the power of the air, the spirit that now worketh in the children of disobedience" (Ephesians 2:2)

That we henceforth be no more children, tossed to and fro, and carried about with every wind of doctrine, by the sleight of men, and cunning craftiness, whereby they lie in wait to deceive. But speaking the truth in love, may grow up into him in all things, which is the head, even Christ. (Ephesians 4:14-15)

The Bible tells us that "All scripture is given by inspiration of God, and is profitable for doctrine, for reproof, for correction, for instruction in righteousness" (2 Timothy 3:16). It further tells us that "No prophecy of the scripture is of any private interpretation" (2 Peter 1:20). When we study the word of the Lord we must do so "Precept upon precept; line upon line, here a little, and there a little" (Isaiah 28:10). We must also learn the art of "Rightly dividing the word of truth" (2 Timothy2:15). Many biblical writers touch on this subject of the doctrine of the air which gives us a better understanding of satan being the prince of the power of the air. Let's look at a few.

The Apostle Paul

In Paul's writing to the church in Corinthians, he gives us details of how he was caught up in the third heaven. This leads us to believe that if there is a third heaven, there must be a first and second heaven. Because a third is only followed in sequential order. (2 Corithians12:2-4). Heavens or heavens realms have different functions. Their operations are determined by their usage in the atmosphere.

The New Testament writer of the book of Hebrews says this in the seventh chapter and in the 26th verse.

"For such a high priest became us, who is holy, harmless, undefiled, separate from sinners, and made higher than the heavens."

This scripture also tells us that there is more than one heaven.

- **The First Heaven:** At the beginning of creation, God said let there be firmament in the midst of the water and let it divide the waters from the firmament. God called the firmament Heaven. This is the sky above the earth. The Latin word for firmament means sky. In this, we see the sun, stars, and the moon. This is the atmosphere right above us. This is also the place where the fowl of the air lives and reigns. This is the cloud that brings forth the elements of the earth (rain, snow, sleet) (Genesis 1:6-8; Genesis 1:7; Psalm 104:12; Deuteronomy 11:11; Psalm 104:12; Isaiah 55:10).
- **The Second Heaven:** This is the place where satan and his evil force dwell. This is the place where spiritual warfare among the angelic host is encountered. In this realm, satan is the prince of the power of the air. The god of this world system. This is the place where the world systems are created. The second heaven is where the devil employs false doctrines and false teachings. It is better known as evil headquarters. (Ephesians 2:2; Ephesians 6:12).
- **The Third Heaven:** This is the place where GOD ALMIGHTY dwells, which is our command center, the Heaven of Heavens. God's Temple. The Bible says, *"Heaven is God's throne, and the earth is his footstool"* (Isaiah 66:1). This is where the Apostle Paul says that he met the Lord in the air.

Satan, as the ruler of the second heaven and the prince of the power of the air, wields influence over the world's system, using it to spread false teachings and doctrines that oppose God's truth. His goal is to deceive humanity into accepting his lies. These false teachings originate in the spiritual realm and are carried through the world's interconnected system, which functions as a network designed to alter the minds and morals of people, steering them away from God's original standard.

The Bible warns against loving the world and its corrupt system, stating, *"If any man loves the world, the love of the Father is not in him"* (1 John 2:15). Satan's system, known as the *cosmos* in Greek, represents the structured order of human government, economics, religion, education, culture, and entertainment—domains he manipulates to spread deception. Through influential figures within this system, he propagates false narratives that oppose truth and righteousness, further corrupting the world's moral and spiritual foundation.

Paul tells the church at Corinth that satan has blinded the minds of unbelievers so they cannot see the glorious gospel of Jesus Christ (2 Corinthians 4:4), for it is the spirit of deception that causes the neon light to shine so bright that they cannot see. A person can have 100% vision in both eyes. However, if a bright light shines directly in your eyes, it will cause temporary blindness. As the god of this world, he uses the spirit of the world to entangle and entrap with lies. It is the same method he has been using since the beginning of time. The Woman said, "*Satan beguiled me,*" which is the telling of a lie.

The only reason a person tells a lie is to deceive. We must understand that any teachings and doctrines directly opposite to the teachings of the Word of God are lies, and their primary purpose is to deceive us. The enemy uses fame, fortune, power, sex, and the love of money to deceive us. All of these are rooted in the three elements of the world. The lust of the eye, the lust of the flesh, and the pride of life. Peter tells us he (satan) is like a roaring lion seeking whom he may devour (1 Peter 5:8). In the book of Job, we see a revealing moment when the sons of God came to present themselves before Him, and satan came along with them. God asked satan where he had been, to which he replied, *"Going to and fro in the earth, and walking up and down in it"* (Job 1:6-7). This reflects satan's ongoing mission—to roam the earth, seeking those he can deceive.

Today, this deception continues through various means, including social media platforms like Twitter, Instagram, TikTok, and Facebook. These platforms often spread ideologies and doctrines that contradict the Word of God, influencing many away from the truth. Satan's strategy remains the same: to use deception to lead people astray.

Hindrances in the Air

And, behold, an hand touched me, which set me upon my knees and upon the palms of my hands. And he said unto me, 'O Daniel, a man greatly beloved, understand the words that I speak unto thee, and stand upright: for unto thee am I now sent.' And when he had spoken this word unto me, I stood trembling. Then said he unto me, 'Fear not, Daniel: for from the first day that thou didst set thine heart to understand, and to chasten thyself before thy God, thy words were heard, and I am come for thy words. But the prince of the kingdom of Persia withstood me one and twenty days: but, lo, Michael, one of the chief princes, came to help me; and I remained there with the kings of Persia.' (Daniel 10:10-13)

In the above scriptures we see there was warfare in the heavenly realms. This, I believe, is the second heaven where satan is the prince of the power of the air. It was in this season that Daniel understood by the books that the children of Israel would only be in Babylon for 70 years, as spoken by the prophet Jeremiah. (Jeremiah 25:11-12)

The first year of the King of Cyrus. Daniel had a vision, and he was puzzled and without understanding. The vision was true, but the time was long. So, he set himself to seek the Lord by prayer and fasting. (Daniel 9:3). God sent the Angel Gabriel to give skill and understanding to Daniel. The word skill and understanding means to provide more clarity. The Bible says, *"If any man lacks wisdom, let him ask of God"* (James 1:5). Daniel was baffled by Jeremiah's prophecy. It is important for us to know that we prophesy in part, and we know in part (1Corinthians13:9-13). God does not always reveal the full meaning or give the full details of the prophecy, but when the Angel Gabriel was sent to the earth realm to Daniel, he experienced what Bible scholars call an *"Angelic Conflict."*

There is a theory that a million years existed between Genesis 1:1 and Genesis 1:2. During this time, satan and his demons participated in a heavenly insurrection by trying to overthrow the established government of God. Since God always responded to sin by judgment, the Bible says that satan and his cohorts were cast down to the earth (Isaiah 14:15, Ezekiel 28:16-18, Revelation 12:9). Jesus says he saw satan falling from Heaven (St. Luke 10:18). Being a former angel, satan had access to the skies (first and second heaven, Job 1:6).

The Mystery in the Air

When Daniel sought the Lord for understanding, Angel Gabriel was sent on the first day to deliver an answer to his prayer, but he was delayed for 21 days due to opposition from the *Prince of Persia.* This reveals the reality of spiritual warfare, where satan attempts to hinder God's plans and deceive believers into thinking their prayers go unanswered. Hindrances often feel like denial, a tactic the enemy uses to create doubt and discourage faith. Even the Apostle Paul faced similar opposition, stating that satan prevented him from visiting the Thessalonian church (1 Thessalonians 2:17-18).

In Daniel's case, the delay occurred in the *second heaven*, where satan operates as the prince of the power of the air. He used a fallen angel—the *Prince of Persia*—to resist Gabriel's mission. This struggle took place during the reign of King Cyrus, who had been prophesied to issue the decree for the Jews to return and rebuild the Temple. Aware of this prophecy, satan fought to block Daniel from receiving divine revelation, knowing that truth brings freedom (St. John 8:32). This passage highlights the unseen battles in the spiritual realm and the importance of perseverance in prayer to overcome the enemy's deception.

As Daniel kept on praying, God sent reinforcement. The Archangel, Micheal, came to aid in the fight. The word *Archangel* means *"Angel of the highest rank.*" Michael is always connected in the Bible as a war angel. For it was Michael who was sent to content with the devil over the body of Moses (Jude 1:9), and it was Michael who fought in the original rebellion and prevailed. (Revelation 12:7) and it will be Michael the Archangel who will set one foot on the sand and one foot on the land. He will blow the trumpet, signifying the beginning of the end, and the dead in Christ will rise first (1 Thessalonians 4:16).

After Gabriel spoke to Daniel to give him an answer to his prayer, he was strengthened and given a better understanding. The angel informed him that he must return to the fight in the air because the Prince of Persia was calling for reinforcement from the Prince of Grecia. The angels were fighting over truth and lies, and the devil was making all efforts to stop man from receiving the truth of God's word. But as Daniel was victorious through his continuous prayer, we too, must always pray (1 Thessalonians 5:17; St Luke 18:1).

The Father of Lies

As we previously studied, satan is known as the father of lies. Adam is known as the father of humanity because he was the first living person on earth. Hippocrates was a Greek physician and philosopher. He is considered the father of medicine for his contributions to the field, such as clinical observation, categorization of diseases, and the formulation of humoral theory. J. Robert Oppenheimer served as the Manhattan Project Los Alamos Laboratory director during World War II. He is called the father of the atomic bomb for his work and role in overseeing the development of the first nuclear weapons, and the list goes on of the fathers of different times, theories, and inventions. The word father denotes a male who begotten an offspring or a male who is the first to accomplish a task so that others can follow. The father is usually the first or head of the family.

A lie is told to deceive and employ an error. Satan, in his acts from the beginning of time, has used deception to cause celestial beings and humanity to become an enemy of God. The spirit of deception's primary purpose is to cause us to lose our right standing with God. God is truth. The Bible tells us, *"It is impossible for God to lie"* (Hebrews 6:18). It further tells us that *"Every good gift and perfect gift come from God" (James 1: 17)*. Satan understands that this is true and that it is God's will for mankind to be free from everything that binds them. He opposes truth by inserting lies to cause men to miss out on God. He has been doing this since the beginning of time and still uses this method today. He is the father of lies.

In the book of St. John, chapter 17. Jesus prays to the Father and says, *"Sanctify them by the truth, your word is truth."* The Bible is the written Word of God. We understand that no prophecy of the scripture is of any private interpretation, and the holy men of old spoke as they were moved by the Holy Ghost (2 Peter 1:20-21). Many were inspired by God to write those things that was revealed to him. As a result, we have a great volume of books that we call the Holy Bible. These things were written and inspired by the Holy Ghost, the third person of the Trinity. They are God-breathed truths which have the ability to heal and deliver humanity. Satan knows this, so he seeks to distort the Word of God and make it of no effect.

As previously mentioned, please allow me to repeat. It is in the air that lies are spoken opposites of the truth (the Word of God). These lies are carried in the waves of wind. Satan employs the systems of the world, which he is the god over, to carry this false wave of winds. Once they are created in the air, the spirit of deception begins to trick key players into introducing them into the earthly realm. They are false teachings (doctrines) carried in the wind.

False Teaching in the Church

The Apostle Paul founded the church of Ephesians on his third missionary journey. In Acts 19:1-2, Paul encountered certain disciples and asked them, *"Have you received the Holy Ghost since you believed?"* They replied, *"We have not heard that there be any Holy Ghost."* When Paul learned that they were baptized only with the baptism of John, he realized they had not yet experienced the fullness of God. Paul, in turn, stayed in Ephesus for three years, teaching and imparting deeper understanding of God's ways, and the church grew strong in its foundation.

However, after Paul's departure, false teachers began to infiltrate the church, spreading deceptive teachings that undermined Paul's instructions. These false teachers used trickery, what the Bible refers to as *"the sleight of men"* and *"cunning craftiness,"* to oppose the truth. These individuals, employed by satan, carried lies meant to be believed and acted upon, leading people astray. Just as satan came in the form of a serpent in the Garden of Eden, he now works through deceived humans to spread falsehoods and disrupt the church's foundation. Jesus tells us in his teaching that the road that leads to eternal life is narrow with few on it. But the road that leads to destruction is wide and broad, and many there are on this road (St. Matthew 7:13).

CHAPTER 5

THE VESSELS OF DECEPTION

"Deception may give us what we want for the present, but it will always take it away in the end." Rachel Hawthorne

Beloved, the Bible makes it very clear that we should know the spirit of error and the spirit of truth. Deception is the tactic that satan uses to cause humanity to lose their right relationship with God. Satan uses vessels of deception to cause men to believe his lies.

> *For such are false apostles, deceitful workers, transforming themselves into the apostles of Christ. And no marvel; for Satan himself is transformed into an angel of light. Therefore, it is no great thing if his ministers also be transformed as the ministers of righteousness; whose end shall be according to their works. (2 Corinthians 11:13-15)*

But in a great house there are not only vessels of gold and of silver, but also of wood and of earth; and some to honor, and some to dishonor. If a man therefore purge himself from these, he shall be a vessel unto honor, sanctified, and meet for the master's use, and prepared unto every good work. (2 Timothy 2:20-21)

For even in the beginning of time, Satan deceived himself and became a prey to his own lie, for in heaven, his name was Lucifer, which means Morning Star. He was the anointed Cherub, but he wanted to be like the Most High. The word of the Lord tells us:

How art thou fallen from heaven, O Lucifer, son of the morning! how art thou cut down to the ground, which didst weaken the nations! For thou hast said in thine heart, I will ascend into heaven, I will exalt my throne above the stars of God: I will sit also upon the mount of the congregation, in the sides of the north: I will ascend above the heights of the clouds; I will be like the Most High. Yet thou shalt be brought down to hell, to the sides of the pit. They that see thee shall narrowly look upon thee and consider thee saying Is this man that made the earth to tremble, that did shake kingdom. (Isaiah 14:12-16)

After satan was brought down to the earth. He still tries to be like God. He established a kingdom on earth that mimics the Kingdom of God. We observe that the Bible talks about the Kingdom of God and the kingdom of satan. As we have learned earlier, satan is;

- The prince of this world
- God of this world's systems
- Prince of the power of the air

In this, we see that satan tries to imitate the Kingdom of God with the kingdom of darkness. The Kingdom of God can be summarized as the everlasting realm where God is sovereign, and Jesus Christ rules forever. The concept of the Kingdom of God is not primarily one of space, territory, or politics but one of kingly rule, reign, and sovereign control.

In the Kingdom of God, we have the Godhead.

- The Father
- The Son
- Holy Ghost

These three are one. Often referred to as the Trinity. In the Kingdom of God, we have angels, also called ministering spirits (Hebrews 1:14). We see in the Kingdom of God that angels have.

- Different rankings
- Different roles

The good angels (elect angels) worship and serve God while also having a role in the world that the Lord created. These angels can be used to bring judgment, and some are used to bring good news. Some angels will have specific tasks in the future, such as the seven angels in charge of sounding the seven trumpets during the tribulation. The Bible tells us that angels worship the Lord and praise Him (Psalm 148:2; Luke 2:13; Hebrews 1:6; Revelation 5:11). Thousands of angels worship the Lord, bringing Him glory (Hebrews 12:22). At certain times, God calls angels to present themselves before Him (Job 1:6; 2:1).

Angels also serve God and carry out His commands (Psalm 103:20). Some of these commands include being sent by God to answer prayers (Daniel) and serve and protect believers (Psalm 34:7; Daniel 6:22; Hebrews 1:14). At times, God can use angels as instruments of judgment on unbelieving and rebellious people and nations (Genesis 19:13; Acts 12:23; Revelation 15:6). Everything that angels do is in accordance with the will of God (Acts 12:23; Revelation 15:6). There are different types of angels with unique roles:

- **Archangels:** These are the highest-ranking angels.
- **Cherubims:** They are involved in the worship and praise of God. After man was expelled from the Garden, the cherubim were used to prevent man from reentering the Garden to gain access to the Tree Of Life. Satan was ranked as a cherubim before his rebellion.
- **Seraphims:** They are the type of angels referred to as fiery ones or serpents. God often sends them as instruments to do His bidding.

Humans are employed in the Kingdom of God. We see that the Lord employs men and women to carry out a special purpose in the earth. These men and women have unique gifts and administration that God gives to them that they may use for his glory.

In the Old Testament, they were listed as

- Kings
- Priests
- Prophets
- And many times, referred to as Servants and Judges.

In the New Testament (Church Age), they are listed as

- **Apostles:** The noun *Apostolos* (ajpovstolo) is a word used in Greek. An ambassador or messenger commissioned to carry out an assignment. Those that are sent out.
- **Prophet:** The word prophet comes from the Hebrew word *nabi* or *nabiy* to bubble forth like a fountain or to utter, speak, or pour forth an announcement. Another word is seer. This gives us the knowledge that this is a person with a special calling and the ability to speak and see by divine inspiration. Beyond what has been spoken or revealed to them in the natural realm, what they see or know is revealed by the Spirit of God.
- **Evangelists:** An evangelist is one who preaches Jesus (the Word of God). An evangelist has the gift of performing miracles, including casting out demons and gifts of healing.
- **Pastors:** The word pastor is derived from the Latin word meaning *Shepherd.* This is one who oversees the flock for its good. The pastor is God's gift to the body of Christ. He is the spiritual overseer for the local church or parish.
- **Teachers:** The teacher is necessary for the body of Christ. For the Lord would not let us be ignorant. It is closely related to the pastor's calling. For the pastor must be able to teach (1 Timothy 3:2).

In all, their primary purpose is to give glory to God in their lives and their works. They are used to express, teach, preach, and proclaim God's word, which is often referred to as *Doctrine*. The doctrine is a teaching derived from the scripture, providing guidance and instruction for faith and practice.

Doctrine encompasses the core theological truths that define and convey the message of faith. Scripture speaks of the Apostles' Doctrine and the Doctrine of Jesus Christ, emphasizing that God inspired men of old to write as they were moved by the Holy Spirit. As stated in the New International Version, *"All Scripture is God-breathed and is useful for teaching."* Additionally, the Bible reminds us that *"The Kingdom of God is not a matter of eating and drinking, but of righteousness, peace, and joy in the Holy Spirit"* (Romans 14:17).

The Kingdom of Darkness

Satan, in his desire to be like God, established his own kingdom on earth after his fall from Heaven. As Revelation 12:12 states, *"Woe to the inhabitants of the earth and the sea! For the devil has come down to you."* However, despite his presence in the earthly realm, satan does not have ultimate control over the earth, for *"The earth is the Lord's, and everything in it"* (Psalm 24:1-2).

Scripture reveals satan's prideful ambition:

- *"I will ascend into heaven."*
- *"I will exalt my throne above the stars of God."*
- *"I will sit upon the mount of the congregation."*
- *"I will ascend above the heights of the clouds."*
- *"I will be like the Most High."*

Although cast down, satan continues his rebellion, establishing a counterfeit kingdom known as the kingdom of darkness, opposing God's righteousness. This contrasts with the Kingdom of God, where *"Let there be light"* (Genesis 1:3) was the first divine command, and Jesus declared, *"I am the Light of the world; in Him, there is no darkness"* (St. John 8:12).

The kingdom of darkness is defined by sin and rebellion (1 John 1:6; 2:11; John 3:19). Satan, as its ruler, opposes all that is holy and righteous. Just as Heaven has ranks of angels, the kingdom of darkness has fallen angels, who were cast down with him after the great war in Heaven (Revelation 12:7-9). Some of these angels are:

- **Principalities and Powers:** These are falling angels and demonic beings. They are ranking leaders in the kingdom of darkness. These spirits rule over princes, governments, states, nations, and communities. These rulings and spirits cover regions. Their presence is felt in cities. These spirits rule over territories.
- **Rulers of the Darkness of this World:** Since satan is the god of this world system and his kingdom is called the kingdom of darkness, this is the ranking spirit that he uses to employ darkness in the world. These spirits are used to cause blindness so that men will not believe the truth of the glorious gospel of Jesus Christ.
- **Spiritual Wickedness:** The Bible makes it very clear that God is a spirit, and those who worship him must worship him in spirit and truth. The spirit realm is a realm that we cannot see in the flesh. In the unseen world, there is a battle going on that affects the world we live in.

The devil employs his demons to fight for the cause of wickedness to prevail in the land. These spirits battle against the goodness of God in the land of the living. So even as God has servants on earth to do his bidding, satan also has servants on earth to do his bidding.

They are called:

- **False Prophets:** This is one whose divine inspiration is not of God but of the devil.
- **False Apostles:** These are those who claim to be God sent. However, they deny any or all truth about the true identity of Jesus Christ. Their work is not in love but rather greed, lust, and power.
- **Deceitful worker:** This is someone who performs the works of Christ but does not live a life of holiness and righteousness. They are deceived into believing that their good deeds alone will grant them entry into Heaven. However, in the end, their faith is placed in works rather than true righteousness.
- **False Christ:** These are those who claim to be the chosen Messiah and deny that Jesus Christ has come in the flesh, but in the real sense, they do not have an authentic anointing.

Even as there are Bible teachings and the Apostle Doctrine of Jesus Christ, satan also employs teachings and doctrines. His teachings are direct opposite of the teachings of the Bible.

They are called:

- **Doctrine of the Devil:** These are teachings that come from satan. They are the lies of the father of lies. They are created to cause men to fall away from the truth of God. This is the falsehood that will cause one to live in a state of apostasy, which is abandonment or violation of faith.
- **Heresy:** A teaching that is contrary to an established doctrine. A dissent of what is believed.

Satan uses false doctrines and heresies to lead people astray, undermine holiness, and keep humanity from eternal life. As the scripture warns:

> *For such are false apostles, deceitful workers, transforming themselves into the apostles of Christ. And no wonder! For Satan himself transforms into an angel of light. Therefore, it is no surprise if his ministers also masquerade as ministers of righteousness; their end will be according to their works. (2 Corinthians 11:13-15)*

Jesus warned us not to be deceived, stating that if it were possible, even the elect would be led astray. The spirit of deception has been present since the beginning of time, first appearing in the earliest days of humanity. Throughout the Bible, this deception has been revealed and confronted. Let's examine a few key examples.

1. In the Days of Moses

In Exodus 7-8, Moses and Aaron confronted Pharaoh, demanding the release of the Israelites. To confirm their message, they performed miracles, which Pharaoh's magicians initially replicated. They turned water into blood and summoned frogs, but their efforts only worsened Egypt's suffering. However, they failed to produce gnats, darkness, or other plagues, proving God's power far greater. As Exodus 10:21 states, *"The LORD said to Moses, stretch out your hand toward heaven, that there may be darkness over Egypt."* Yet, in the midst of darkness, Israel dwelt in light, revealing that God's kingdom is of light, while satan's is of darkness. Other chapters highlighting God's work through Moses are Exodus 8:16-19 and Exodus 10:10-23.

2. The Prophet of the Old Testament

> *If there arise among you a prophet, or a dreamer of dreams, and giveth thee a sign or a wonder, And the sign or the wonder come to pass, whereof he spake unto thee, saying, 'Let us go after other gods, which thou hast not known, and let us serve them;' Thou shalt not hearken unto the words of that prophet, or that dreamer of dreams: for the Lord your God proved you, to know whether ye love the Lord your God with all your heart and with all your soul. (Deuteronomy 13:1-3)*

In these verses, we see that a prophet or dreamer may give a sign or wonder, and it may come to pass. However, the fulfillment of a prophecy alone does not confirm that the prophet is truly sent by God. Many assume that supernatural insight is the mark of divine anointing, but the Scripture teaches otherwise. If a prophet or dreamer leads people to serve other gods—note that *"god"* is lowercase in the King James Version, signifying false gods—then their actions contradict righteousness and holiness.

The Bible warns us not to follow such individuals, as this is God's way of testing our faithfulness. *"You shall love the Lord your God with all your heart, soul, and mind"* (St. Matthew 22:37), and *"You shall have no other gods before Me"* (Exodus 20:3). God is a jealous God and will not take second place. As taught in Pentecostal tradition, *"If He is not God of all, He will not be God at all."* The devil can imitate miracles, but he cannot live holy. These verses remind us that God is proving us—will we follow a prophecy that comes to pass, or will we remain faithful to the true and living God?

3. The Ministry of Jesus

> *"For many shall come in my name, saying, I am Christ; and shall deceive many." (St. Matthew 24:5)*

The word Christ means anointed one. Many will feel that they will be okay because they have been anointed. We must remember that God chooses to use people at his will. The Bible tells us that Christ is sometimes preached for reasons other than the truth. "*What then? notwithstanding, every way, whether in pretense, or in truth, Christ is preached; and I therein do rejoice, yea, and will rejoice*" (Philippians 1:18). We must understand that religion is a big business. Many do it for fame, fortune, and the love of money. When ministry is not being done for the love of God and the love of his people, it is false work. Therefore, anything false is not of God. This has become a common deception from satan, for the ministry of Jesus was to do the will of God.

4. False Teaching

False teaching has become so common that many are buying into the lie and deception of its practices. False teaching has been widely accepted as truth because we fail to be students of the word ourselves. However, we are deceived by what sounds good and pleasant to the ear. The Bible tells us, "The time will come when men will not tolerate sound doctrine, but with itching ears, they will gather around themselves teachers to suit their own desires" (2 Timothy 4:3).

In this day and age, false things will be accepted as authentic. Men who do not want to change from their evil ways have been deceived.

However, we must understand that "Faith comes by hearing and hearing by the word" (Romans 10:17). Without faith, it is impossible to please God. We must further understand that the Bible says, "We shall know the truth, and the truth will make us free" (St. John 8:32). The enemy of our soul employs false teachings to make us unpleasing to God, causing us to be bound in our sins and block our ears from hearing the truth that would lead to eternal life.

5. Our Response to False Teaching

But though we, or an angel from heaven, preach any other gospel unto you than that which we have preached unto you, let him be accursed. As we said before, so say I now again, If any man preach any other gospel unto you than that ye have received, let him be accursed. For do I now persuade men, or God? or do I seek to please men? for if I yet pleased men, I should not be the servant of Christ. But I certify you, brethren, that the gospel which was preached of me is not after man. For I neither received it of man, neither was I taught it, but by the revelation of Jesus Christ. (Galatians 1: 8-12)

In the above verses, the Apostle Paul speaks to the church in Galatia, which scholars believe was likely the first book he wrote. Founded during Paul's first missionary journey, the church was built on the message of salvation by grace, not by works—a revelation he received directly from Jesus Christ. However, false teachers had infiltrated the church, distorting the gospel and leading believers astray through deception.

Paul issues a strong warning: If anyone, even an angel, preaches a different gospel, let them be accursed. This serves as a timeless reminder for all believers to remain faithful to the true gospel and reject any false teachings.

CHAPTER 6

How Shall We Know Them

"Truth is powerful, and it prevails." Sojourner Truth

Jesus taught that **a tree is known by the fruit it bears.** Just as children often reflect the traits of their parents—whether biological or adopted—believers should reflect the nature of God.

> *"For a good tree does not bear bad fruit, nor does a bad tree bear good fruit. For every tree is known by its own fruit. For men do not gather figs from thorns, nor do they gather grapes from a bramble bush." (St. Luke 6:43-44)*

Throughout the Scripture, the life of a believer is compared to a tree. The fig tree represents Israel, and Psalm 1:2-3 describes the righteous as *"A tree planted by rivers of water, prospering in all they do."*

Jesus told His disciples, "*I am the vine; you are the branches. If you abide in Me, you will bear much fruit.*" Just as an apple tree produces apples and a pear tree produces pears, God's children must bear His characteristics. God is holy, righteous, and full of light—He has no darkness or falsehood in Him. Therefore, as His children, we are called to reflect His holiness, truth, and righteousness.

Not By Work

The church of Galatia had heard the word of salvation by grace and not by work. For grace is the unmerited favor of God. *"Let no man say they are saved by work lest any man should boast"* (Ephesians 2:9). In the Scripture, we see that many performed work, but yet they missed the mark. The devil deceives people into believing that their actions alone make them right with God. However, the Bible makes it clear that those who are false will have works but lack a true, righteous lifestyle. In the end, their deeds alone will define them, but not their relationship with God.

Work Vs. a Holy Lifestyle

As I continue my commentary on the spirit of deception. I want to bring to light how we can know that something or someone is of God and not of God.

> *Not everyone that saith unto me, 'Lord, Lord,' shall enter into the kingdom of heaven; but he that doeth the will of My Father which is in heaven. Many will say to me in that day, 'Lord, Lord, have we not prophesied in thy name? and in thy name have cast out devils? And in*

thy name done many wonderful works?' And then will I profess unto them, I never knew you: depart from me, ye that work iniquity. (St. Matthew 7:21-23)

"Blessed are the pure in heart: for they shall see God." (St. Matthew 5:8)

As stated throughout the pages of this book, the Bible makes it very clear we should know the spirit of error and the spirit of truth. One of the primary ways satan employs deception is through a vessel that has been deceived. Anyone who has been deceived has the ability to deceive others. In the above verse, the Bible tells the story of the finale of one's life. We see that they performed many mighty works in the name of the Lord. They had the ability to do it.

However, at the end of life, when it was time for them to stand before the Lord. They were not granted access to a heavenly reward. In their dissent, they ask about the mighty work they had performed. The Lord said, *"I never knew you. You worker of iniquity."*

What Is Iniquity

"Nevertheless, the foundation of God standeth sure, having this seal, The Lord knoweth them that are His. And, let every one that nameth the name of Christ depart from iniquity." (2 Timothy 2:19)

It is said that the Hebrew word used most often for iniquity means *"a deep-rooted sin."* This is a sin of the heart that has grown over time, and now there is no more remorse. I have often heard this is a hidden sin that no one knows of but God and the person.

The workers of miracles in the above verse become so comfortable with the sin of the heart that they no longer ask God to take it out of their lives. It became embroiled in their fiber. It was who they were and who they had become. They became so comfortable with this sin. It is because of iniquity, which is a form of deception. God is a righteous God, and iniquity is not a part of His DNA nor the DNA of His children. So, these workers were deceived to perform miracles with iniquity in their lives. This deception causes them to miss heavenly rewards.

The Pure in Heart

The pure in heart are blessed—not only in this life but also in eternity, as they will see God. This should be the ultimate goal of every believer. 1 Peter 3:4 reminds us to guard our inner being and not let it become corrupt.

The spirit of deception in the world today seeks to lead people astray, causing them to sin against God and lose their true identity as His children. Its purpose is to rob humanity of its divine calling and prevent them from reaching heaven. True men and women of God are recognized not by their works alone but by their righteous lives.

CHAPTER 7

The Power of Knowledge

"My people are destroyed for lack of knowledge; because thou hast rejected knowledge, I will also reject thee." (Hosea 4:6)

As we have learned, the opposite of a lie is truth. The Bible tells us that God is the *TRUE* and living God, for it is impossible for God to lie (Hebrews 6:18). He holds His word above His name (Psalm 138:2). The knowledge of truth is our greatest weapon to combat the lies of the enemy. However, truth can only be obtained with knowledge, and knowledge comes through hard work. The Bible says that my people are destroyed by a lack of knowledge. This tells us that God uses knowledge to protect us and preserve us from ruins.

The Apostle Paul, in speaking to the church at Thessalonica, says, *"I would not you be ignorant brethren"* (1 Thessalonians 4:13). Paul also says the same thing to the church at Corinth concerning spiritual gifts (1 Corinthians 12:1). Paul knew that being unlearned of truth would cause defeat, as the devil's primary mission is to have the human race unable to discern between right and wrong. Satan knows what God has to offer will bring greater value to your life and lineage. He knows that if mankind chooses truth over error, their lives will be richer in unknowable and untold ways.

To prevent this, satan uses the spirit of deception to blind people from seeking wisdom and knowledge. Have you ever noticed that distractions arise when you set your heart on seeking God? Or that when you pick up your Bible, sleepiness overtakes you? These are deliberate tactics of the enemy, designed to hinder knowledge and create spiritual blindness. His goal is to send a strong form of delusion, as the scripture says, *"When we would do good, evil is always present"* (Romans 7:21).

Wisdom and Knowledge

For us to better understand wisdom and knowledge, we must study their meanings through the lens of the Scripture.

- **Wisdom:** It is defined in the Old Testament as the Hebrew word "*hokmiah.*" This refers to a skill or ability imparted by the Spirit of God. In the New Testament, we see the Hebrew word "*sophia.*" This refers to wisdom as a gift of God given to specific individuals in order to equip them to live a godly life. It denotes divine wisdom with knowledge, intelligence, and understanding.
- **Knowledge:** This is defined biblically as the Hebrew word "*epiginosko.*" This refers to a person's understanding of God and

His son, an awareness of His will for one's life, and an intimate relationship with Him.

The Apostle Paul

In the book of Ephesians, the Apostle Paul prays that God would grant the church the spirit of wisdom and revelation in the knowledge of Jesus Christ. He further desires that the eyes of our understanding be enlightened. Previously, we learned that satan blinds the minds of people so they cannot see the glorious Gospel of Christ. To combat this, Paul emphasizes the need for wisdom and revelation, which is revealed by the Spirit of God rather than human reasoning.

When Jesus asked His disciples, *"Who do men say that I am?"* Many responded with logical answers based on perception. However, Peter received divine revelation, declaring, *"Thou art the Christ, the Son of the living God."* Jesus affirmed this by saying, *"Blessed art thou, Simon Barjona: for flesh and blood hath not revealed it unto thee"* (Matthew 16:17). Living by revelational knowledge brings blessings, as the Spirit of God leads us toward success and clarity. The Psalmist prayed, *"Lord, lead me in a plain path because of my enemy"* (Psalm 27:11), affirming that God makes truth clear to His people. Paul recognized that this wisdom was essential for the church to avoid being ignorant of satan's schemes.

The Apostle Paul says he prayed for the church of Ephesus that they would have the spirit of wisdom and knowledge. The Bible says, *"Ask, and it will be given to you; seek, and you will find: knock, and it will be opened to you"* (St. Matthew 7:7).

The Proverbs

In the book of Proverbs, we are told, *"The fear of the Lord is the beginning of wisdom, and the knowledge of the holy is understanding"* (Proverbs 9:10). One must have reverential respect for the Lord to start the process of imparted wisdom and knowledge from above. This is the first requirement. To receive divine wisdom, one must be committed to their salvation and walk with God.

Additionally, we are told in the book of Proverbs that: *"Wisdom is the principal thing; therefore, get wisdom and with all thy getting get understanding"* (Proverbs 4:7). The writer of the Proverbs lists many of the attributes of wisdom. Please see below:

- If we exalt her, she will promote us
- If we embrace her, she will bring honor to us
- She shall give our head an ornament of grace
- A crown of glory shall she deliver to us
- If we receive her. She adds years to our life.

In the book of Proverbs, the writer emphasizes the importance of having the spiritual endowment of the gift of wisdom and knowledge. For godly wisdom and knowledge only come from above, not as the wisdom of this world.

The Wisdom from Above Vs. Worldly Wisdom

The Bible makes it very clear that there is wisdom from above and from the world.

Wisdom from Above

> *"But the wisdom that is from above is first pure, then peaceable, gentle, and easy to be intreated, full of mercy and good fruits, without partiality, and without hypocrisy." (James 3:17)*

The wisdom from above is first pure. In His Sermon on the Mount, Jesus teaches His followers, *"Blessed are the pure in heart, for they shall see God."* He knew that one of the virtues of pure religion is to keep oneself unspotted from the world (the cosmos). In the above scripture, we find many fruits of the spirit. Love, joy, peace, patience, kindness, goodness, faithfulness, gentleness, self-control. (Galatians 5:22-23). When the wisdom from above is in the believer's life, he will demonstrate the fruits of the Holy Spirit because he is connected to the true vine.

Worldly Wisdom

> *"But the wisdom that descendeth not from above but is earthly, sensual, devilish." (James 3:15)*

In this passage, James warns that there is a way that seems right in our own eyes but is not of God. The wisdom that comes from being wise in our own eyes is inspired by the spirit of deception. The term *earthly* refers to the world (cosmos), where satan is the god of this worldly system. This worldly wisdom directly opposes the Word of God and is rooted in physical, carnal, fleshly, and sensual teachings. These are the fleeting pleasures of the world, which the Bible says are temporary. The wisdom of the world is a tool satan uses to trap us and steal the joy of a rich life in Christ, leaving us empty and unfulfilled.

Godly wisdom, however, is first pure, which means that worldly wisdom is impure and unclean, coming from a corrupt source intended to contaminate. The word *devilish* refers to the traits and actions of the devil, who comes to steal, kill, and destroy. This is the wisdom from the world, originating from the devil. We are encouraged to *"Set our affection on things above, not on things on the earth"* (Colossians 3:2).

Having distinguished between worldly wisdom and wisdom from above, let us now focus on the spirit of wisdom and knowledge. These gifts must be imparted to our spirit, mind, and heart so that we are not prey to the strong delusions in the world today. Wisdom and knowledge come from above, from the mighty God. They are special gifts given to believers who ask with diligence. As Jesus promised, *"It is your Father's good pleasure to give you the kingdom"* (St. Luke 12:32). He will not withhold anything good from us, and as a father delights in giving good gifts to his children, God desires to give us His wisdom and knowledge. As I grew in my walk with God, this truth became clearer to me through prayer and reflection on the Scripture.

Proverbs 2:3-6 says,

> *Yea, if thou criest after knowledge, and liftest up thy voice for understanding; If thou seekest her as silver, and searchest for her as for hid treasures; Then shalt thou understand the fear of the LORD, and find the knowledge of God. For the LORD giveth wisdom: out of His mouth cometh knowledge and understanding.*

In the above passage, the writer of Proverbs tells us that this special endowment will only be given to one who is diligent and persistent. The writer tells us this is a hidden treasure that must be found.

Jesus teaches in St. Matthew 13:44-45 that the kingdom of heaven is like a hidden treasure and a pearl of great price—things of immense value that must be sought after with diligence. Likewise, divine wisdom and knowledge do not come easily; they require effort and a deep desire to seek God. Proverbs compares wisdom to silver, a rare and precious metal in ancient Israel, emphasizing that true wisdom is not for everyone but is given to those who pursue it earnestly.

The Bible assures us that *"God is a rewarder of them that diligently seek him"* (Hebrews 11:6). The Greek word *"harus"* signifies determination and zeal, reflecting the necessity of persistent pursuit. Jesus confirms this by saying, *"Blessed are they which do hunger and thirst after righteousness: for they shall be filled"* (St. Matthew 5:6). Proverbs further reinforces the importance of diligence, stating that the diligent will be enriched (Proverbs 10:4, 13:4) and must guard their hearts with vigilance (Proverbs 4:23). Seeking the spirit of wisdom and knowledge requires unwavering commitment and sacrifice.

As I dedicated myself to prayer, fasting, and studying the Scripture during my early ministry, I fervently asked God for the spirit of wisdom and knowledge. Despite opposition from some church leaders who misunderstood my intentions, I remained steadfast in my pursuit. I understood that seeking divine wisdom was a labor of love and persistence. Years later, during my ordination process, God granted me a vision where I felt a heavy, warm coat placed upon me, and I heard the words, *"You asked for it."* From that moment, my ministry transformed, and I began to connect Scriptures with ease, guided by divine wisdom.

The Bible declares, *"The Word of God is quick, and powerful, and sharper than any two-edged sword... and is a discerner of the thoughts and intents of the heart"* (Hebrews 4:12). When we pursue God's wisdom, He sharpens our discernment and equips us to navigate life with clarity and power. The spirit of wisdom and knowledge is not just intellectual understanding—it is a divine gift that allows believers to perceive truth, avoid deception, and walk in the fullness of God's purpose.

"... And His name was called the Word of God."
(Revelation 19:13)

Study, Study, Study

When I was a young man in the church, there was a saint I deeply admired—a Prophetess known for her prophetic utterances. I often sought her counsel and prayers. One day, in prayer, she gave me a word from the Lord. That I shall never forget, she said, *"Brother Byron, the Lord is telling me to tell you to Study, Study, Study."* We have always been told that when the Lord says something more than once, there is emphasis being placed on it. Today, I truly say that I am glad that I obeyed that word and became a student of the Word of God.

As we study the word of the Lord closely, we understand that God the Father, Jesus the Son, and the Holy Spirit are one. They eternally existed in one person. John the Beloved Apostle, later known as John the Revelator, was given his testimony on the Isle of Patmos. In the 19th chapter of the book of Revelation, he is given a vision by the angels of God. One of the things he is allowed to see is that in heaven, Jesus' name was *THE WORD OF GOD.*

This is in accordance with John's earlier writings. The gospel book that bears his name informs us of the same. John writes that, *"In the beginning was the Word, and the Word was with God, and the Word was God."* He goes on to tell us that the Word was made flesh and dwelt among us, and we beheld His glory, the glory of the only begotten of the Father. John makes a divine connection that Jesus Christ and *THE WORD OF GOD* is one. When John the Apostle was the elder statesman of the church, he wrote the same. *"For there are three that bear record in heaven the Father, the Word and the Holy Ghost: and these three are one"* (1 John 5:7).

Therefore, you can never separate God from His Word because they are one. The Bible consists of writings from holy men who were divinely inspired to speak and record God's message. That same Spirit commanded them to write their words in a book. For the Holy Spirit will only testify of Jesus Christ.

When we are void of understanding of the Word of God, we lack the knowledge to combat the spirit of our time, which is the spirit of deception. That is why we are encouraged to follow on to know the Lord. We must study His words and cry out for His knowledge day and night. To meditate and delight ourselves in the law of the Lord, as David said, *"Thy word have I hidden in my heart that I might not sin against thee"* (Psalm 119:11). For a persistent search for wisdom and knowledge will yield great results.

CHAPTER 8

A Strong Delusion

"Should the believer neglect the teaching of the Bible, failing to watch and pray even though trusting his pure motive to keep him from deception, he shall be deceived." Watchman Nee

One of the many manifestations of the spirit of deception in the earthly realm is a strong delusion. The scripture below states that God is the sender of such a delusion. However, when we dedicate ourselves to understanding the ways of the Lord, we come into full awareness of His truth. The Bible declares that all souls belong to the Lord and that He is not willing for any to perish but desires that all come to repentance. His patience with humanity is great, as He longs for all to embrace the truth.

> *"And for this cause, God shall send them strong delusion, that they should believe a lie."* (2 Thessalonians 2:11)

God's love for humanity is so profound that He promised the end would not come until the gospel was preached throughout the entire world. Jesus commanded His followers to go into all the world and share the good news. The Bible also tells us that faith comes by hearing, and hearing by the Word of God (Romans 10:17). Once a person hears the Word and comes to the knowledge of the truth, they must embrace it by faith. As previously discussed, when one rejects knowledge, God, in turn, rejects them.

A delusion is a false belief that appears to be true but is, in reality, a lie. Such deception takes hold when one rejects the truth of God's Word.

A Lying Spirit

The spirit of deception lurks with the intent to mislead, aligning with satan, the father of lies. Lies exist to deceive, as seen in the Old Testament account of King Ahab. Ahab, who did evil in the sight of the Lord, rejected the word of a true prophet and instead embraced the counsel of 400 false prophets. His heart was so hardened that he preferred lies over truth.

Despite multiple warnings, Ahab refused to accept God's truth. As a result, God declared, *"Because you have rejected knowledge, I will reject you."* In executing judgment, God allowed a fallen spirit to act as a lying spirit in the mouths of the false prophets. This deception ultimately led to Ahab's downfall, demonstrating how rejecting truth opens the door to delusion and divine judgment.

The word of the Lord tells us, *"It is a terrible thing to fall in the hand of the living God"* (Hebrews 10:31). If we continually reject the sovereign God, a time will come when there is no longer an opportunity to return or repent. Remember, *"Those that reject the knowledge of God he will reject them"* (Hosea 4:6).

In This Last Day

As we witness the signs of the Lord's return, it becomes evident that evil is spreading rapidly throughout the earth. Knowing his time is short, the devil is working tirelessly to deceive and corrupt. A great rebellion against God's laws and principles is taking place, as many reject established truths in favor of sinful pleasures. As a result, God allows a strong delusion to infiltrate the earth. When individuals come to the knowledge of truth but reject it, they become susceptible to the spirit of deception. This spirit blinds them, causing them to believe lies as if they were truth. The book of Romans warns about those who inherit God's wrath because they suppress the truth in unrighteousness, choosing sin over righteousness. As James 4:17 states, *"For he that knows to do good and does it not, to him it is sin."*

Those who have known the truth must be especially vigilant. Many recognize God as the true and living God and hear the gospel of Jesus Christ, yet fail to honor Him. Over time, their thoughts become futile, and their hearts grow darkened (Romans 1:21; Ephesians 4:18). This spiritual decline occurs when individuals neglect to renew their minds with God's Word, allowing worldly desires to take hold. The Bible explicitly warns, *"They failed to retain the knowledge of God"* (Romans 1:28). Because of this rejection, God gives them over to their own ways. Their refusal to remain in the light leads them into spiritual blindness, distancing them from God's truth.

In the professional world, maintaining knowledge is essential for effectiveness. As a healthcare administrator, I must stay updated with industry standards to remain compliant. Likewise, believers must continually nurture their relationship with God to retain His knowledge. However, as Romans 1:22-25 states, when people fail to keep their faith current, God allows them to follow their own desires, leading to deception. Paul expands on this in 2 Thessalonians 2:10, explaining that they were given over to sin because they rejected the love of the truth. The spirit of deception convinces them that judgment will never come, keeping them in spiritual bondage. They walk in darkness, practicing sin without remorse. Yet, redemption is still possible—if they return to the knowledge of the truth, they can be saved.

CHAPTER 9

The Great Spiritual Reversion

"Beloved, these are the last days, and men are falling every day and in every way." Byron K. Parker

The Apostle Paul, in his writing in what bible scholars often refer to as *"The Pauline Letters."* Describes a time before the return of the Lord Jesus Christ; there would be a great reversal of the faith. It is commonly known as backsliding and sometimes referred to as falling away or departing from the faith.

> *"Now the Spirit speaketh expressly, that in the latter times some shall depart from the faith, giving heed to seducing spirits, and doctrines of devils." (1 Timothy 4:1)*

> *"Let no man deceive you by any means: for that day shall not come, except there come a falling away first, and that man of sin be revealed, the son of perdition."* (2 Thessalonians 2:3)

The Bible gives us an illustration of how this is accomplished. This is not new to the students of the Word of God, for we read in Old Testament times that, on many occasions, the children of Israel went backward. *"Setting down to eat and rose up to play turning aside quickly"* (Exodus 32:6-8).

But we understand that this would be an epidemic among Christian circles in the latter days. Men and women will choose to return to a life that displeases God, just as a dog returns to its vomit (Proverbs 26:11; 2 Peter 2:22). As seen in the verse above, this is made possible by the spirit of deception. When someone who has come into the knowledge of truth abandons it for a lie, it is clear they have been deceived.

The devil employs two ancient spirits to infiltrate the lives of believers—seduction and deception. These twin spirits work together, using the same old tactics to lead people astray. Like an old dog with an old trick, the enemy continues to lure believers away from the truth, ensnaring them in spiritual blindness.

Seducing Spirit

My mother often said, *"Satan will paint you a pretty picture and make you think the grass is greener on the other side."* He does this to lure you into traps to cause you to miss out on God. Throughout the pages of the Scripture, we see the work of the seducing spirit. This is the spirit that draws you to the well to drink the poison. The seducing spirit works in connection with man's own uncensored and untamed lust. The book of James tells us. "*Every man is tempted when he is drawn away of his own lust and enticed*" (James 1:14).

To fully grasp this, we must understand that man is three-dimensional—he is a spirit (Ecclesiastes 12:7), he lives in a body (1 Corinthians 6:18), and he has a soul (Mark 8:37). When we surrender our lives to Christ, we are made new creatures (2 Corinthians 5:17). While we have the promise of bodily redemption (Romans 8:23), we must constantly contend with the soul—the seat of our emotions, thoughts, and desires. If this part of us is not surrendered to Christ and governed by His Word, we become vulnerable to deception.

The enemy of our soul uses the seducing spirit to lure believers away from God. This spirit exploits our emotions, fleshly desires, and distractions, leading us away from the truth. When satan succeeds in drawing us away, he systematically drains us of our joy, which is our strength. As we grow weaker, we become spiritually fatigued, unable to resist his attacks.

Once we are weakened, satan introduces the spirit of deception, which replaces God's truth with *"doctrines of the devil"*—false teachings meant to distort our faith and lead us further into darkness. If we fail to guard our souls and renew our minds with the Word of God, we risk falling into this trap. However, by remaining rooted in Christ, we can resist these spirits and walk in the truth of God's Word.

The Twin Spirits in the Life of Samson

When we study the life of Samson, we see the work of the twin spirits that cause one to fall away from the faith. One draws him, and the other captures him through deceit.   Samson was chosen from his birth to serve the Lord as a Nazarite. For the children of Israel did evil again in the sight of the Lord. And the Lord delivered them over into the hands of the Philistines for 40 years.

Consequently, the children of Israel cried out unto the Lord, and God rose Samson to deliver them out of the hands of the Philistines. As a child, Samson grew up under the guidance and tutelage of godly parents. The Spirit of the Lord began to move on him at the camp of Dan. But yet Samson is like us. All members of the human race inherited a sinful nature from our father, Adam. This must be put under subjection. It was not Samson's fault. This is a battle that all mankind must contend with.

The Bible says Samson went down to Timnath and saw a woman, one of the daughters of the Philistines. In this, we see the seducing spirit moving in a time of innocence. It is normal for a young man to be interested in a young woman. However, man must modify his interest so that it will not be in a restricted place, just like Eve. There was nothing wrong with Eve desiring more knowledge, but satan drew her away to cause her to desire it from a restricted place.

Bear in mind that God has always placed restrictions on man. Please allow me to highlight that God chose Samson to do exploits. The more God's hand is on you, the more you will have to live a life of restriction. *"For unto whomsoever much is given, of him shall be much required"* (St. Luke 12:48). Throughout Samson's life, he struggled with misplaced emotions and desire. The seducing spirit kept trying until it drew him into a place where the deceiving spirit was able to entrap him. Samson became what I call a *"casualty of deceit."* We must understand it's an ongoing fight. The enemy may leave you for a season, as in the life of Jesus. But he will be back. Please take note that the devil only resists steadfastness in the faith (1 Peter 5:9).

The Twin Spirits in the Life of David

In a very familiar story, we see the twin spirits at work in David's life. In a time of spiritual idleness, God destined David to be a warrior after his long descension with Saul. David has now ascended to the king's throne, and the nation is at war. King David is sitting idle at home, and as he looks out, he sees beautiful Bathsheba bathing. The twin spirits immediately go to work. The beauty of the woman bathing causes David to enquire about her.

King David finds out that she is the daughter of Eliam and the wife of Uriah the Hittite who is at battle. King David calls for the woman and lies with her. This takes place during the time of conception, and David finds out that Bathsheba is pregnant. He sends for Uriah from the battlefield and commands him to go home and be with his wife. Uriah was so committed to the war that he refused to go home.

King David plots the murder of Uriah all in an attempt to cover his sin. The seducing spirit comes to David and draws him to lie with another man's wife. The deceiving spirit makes David think that he can come up with the perfect plot to get away with the perfect murder. But this spirit lied to the King. Because the eyes of the Lord are in every place, beholding the evil and the good (Proverbs 15:3). The Bible further tells us that your sin will surely find you (Numbers 32:32).

The Engrafted Word of God

Paul warns Timothy that the seducing and deceiving spirits will be at an all-time high in the last days, working relentlessly to lead people away from the faith. These two spirits serve as gateways for evil forces in the world. However, the answer to overcoming them is always found in the Word of God.

In a time of great deception, intense spiritual battles, and powerful forces at work, God provides healing through the *"balm in Gilead"* for the nations (Jeremiah 46:11). The Word of God is magnified, and in the Book of Hebrews, we are given insight into God's last-days strategy. The writer explains that while God once spoke through the prophets, in these final days, He has sent His Son, Jesus Christ, who is the living Word (Hebrews 1:1-2; St. John 1:14).

James further emphasizes that the engrafted Word of God has the power to save our souls. Since the seducing spirit seeks to attach itself to the soulish nature of man, we must cut it off at the root by firmly planting God's Word in our hearts. When something is engrafted, it becomes an inseparable part of us—just as my childhood pastor used to say, *"Get a bulldog hold on God."* The Word of God must be applied to our emotions, feelings, and thoughts to stand strong against deception (James 1:21).

CHAPTER 10

A LIGHT IN DARKNESS

"Our darkest moments give us the opportunity for the seasons of our greatest growth." Justin Farley

John the Beloved Apostle, in his earlier writing, often described himself as "The disciple whom Jesus loved" or "The beloved disciple." He writes his letter about the life, times, and ministry of Jesus Christ in the third person (The Gospel According to John).

> *"I am the light of the world. Whoever follows me will not walk in darkness but will have the light of life." (St. John 8:12)*

His writings are so unique that many of his insights are not recorded in the Synoptic Gospels. It is said that John is the youngest of all the other disciples. John is recorded as being in the inner circle of Jesus. He was invited to the Mount of Transfiguration along with Peter and James (St Matthew 17:1-13; St Mark 9:2-13; St Luke 9:28-36). We read that at times, John would lean on the bosom of Jesus (St. John 13:23, 20:2). John has a great deal of love for the Savior, and because of his closeness to Jesus, he sees things that the other disciples did not see and shares them in his writings. Out of all the attributes that he ascribes to Jesus, for our commentary, let's focus on Jesus being the Light of the World.

Light and Darkness

As we read in Genesis, God is the creator of light and darkness. "For the Earth was without form and void and darkness covered the face of the earth, and the Spirit of God moved on the face of the earth, and God said let there be Light. Light He called Day, and Darkness He called Night" (Genesis 1:2-5). In this, God is making a distinct difference between the two. He separates them, and each has a divine purpose in the will of God. Throughout the chronicles of the Scripture, light and darkness are contrary to one another, and they are rivals. Let's look at a few.

"Woe to those who call evil good and good evil, who put darkness for light and light for darkness, who put bitter for sweet and sweet for bitter!" (Isaiah 5:20)

"Rejoice not over me, O my enemy; when I fall, I shall rise; when I sit in darkness, the Lord will be a light to me." (Micah 7:8)

"For you are all children of light, children of the day. We are not of the night or of the darkness." (1 Thessalonians 5:5)

In the above verses, the word darkness means *choshek (kho-shek)* in Hebrew, meaning misery, destruction, death, ignorance, sorrow, and obscurity.

Light in Hebrew means victory, justice, righteousness, and guidance. To walk in the light is to live by God's known standards.

In each of these, we see that light and darkness are opposers. Light is described as good, and darkness as evil.

John starts his gospel by informing us that Jesus was present at the very beginning of eternity and time. He let his audience know that Jesus was the Word, and the Word was one with God. The Word that was spoken at creation becomes light in the darkness, shining away the darkness. The darkness did not comprehend the light. Mostly, people tend not to respond positively to what they do not understand. It was in the life of Jesus that the Bible says He was in the world, and He created the world. Yet the world did not know Him. He came to His own, and His own did not receive Him. John describes Jesus as being the Light and the Word. These two are one, and they work simultaneously.

As Jesus is the Light, He commands His children to walk of light (Ephesians 5:8-9). To walk of something is to model the pattern that has been laid. For the fruit of the light is all goodness, righteousness, and truth. Consequently, light is the opposite of darkness. Jesus is the Light, and satan is the darkness. Satan filled the world with darkness using the spirit of deception. In darkness, you cannot see clearly, and you cannot visualize the dangers that are in your path. Darkness causes one to have a great disadvantage. Darkness is how the enemy ultimately gains access to our lives by keeping us blind so that we cannot see. God, in His love for humanity, sent Jesus into the world to undo the work of satan (1 John 3:8). Jesus was the Light that shines in darkness. The only thing that can overturn darkness is light. Light reproves the work of darkness (Ephesians 5:1).

Children of the Light

The primary purpose of this volume is to help believers rediscover true light in a dark world as we have come to understand that satan fills the world with lies and deceptions, all in an attempt to cause men to walk in darkness so they cannot see the glorious gospel.

Jesus came into the world to be the Light of the World. John tells us that Jesus is the Word of God. However, we are commanded to be children of the light. If we are to fulfill this mandate, we must walk and live our life according to the Word of God. For the Word of God is the only thing that can shine brighter than the darkness of satan and expose the deception of the night of darkness. Light and darkness are contrary to one another and the children of the light will not be understood and often not received.

The original state of the world was formless, void, and covered in darkness, reflecting the spiritual condition of humanity. The Psalmist acknowledges this by saying, *"I was shapen in iniquity, and in sin did my mother conceive me"* (Psalm 51:5), while Paul affirms, *"In my flesh dwelleth no good thing"* (Romans 7:18). From the very beginning, man was deceived in his innocence, which is why we are commanded to be transformed by the renewing of our minds and not to conform to the world, for the world remains in darkness (Romans 12:2).

Instead, we are called to be children of the Light, aligning our thoughts with God's Word, for deception is an agent of darkness. As the Psalmist declares, *"Thy word is a lamp unto my feet and a light unto my path"* (Psalm 119:105). Jesus further instructs His followers, *"Ye are the light of the world. A city that is set on a hill cannot be hid"* (St. Matthew 5:14). Just as a light shining in darkness becomes the focus, God's people are His showcase to the world. Only when light is turned on do things become clear, and in the same way, we are called to let our light shine amid darkness to glorify God.

The Purpose of Darkness

As previously mentioned, darkness has a purpose. God did not rid the world of darkness. However, he separated light and darkness. I believe this is because God, in His infinite wisdom, knows that darkness would play a vital role in the development of His overall plan. Darkness would serve as *"In all things working together for the good of them that love the Lord."* It would be the defining that distinguishes true light. This would help us know right from wrong, truth from lies, and false from real.

In the ministry of Jesus, He chose 12 men to train and impart spiritual values and traits. They would be the ones who would later tell His story. They would write about His teaching and deeds. These men were fishermen, business owners, and tax collectors hand-picked by Jesus—yet among them was a thief. Even darkness serves a purpose.

At the beginning of creation, God made two great lights. The greater light to rule the day (sun), and the lesser light to rule the night (moon and stars), thereby dividing the light from the darkness. *"And God saw that it was good" (Genesis 1:16-18).* In darkness, God placed a ruling light. This light is there to show forth the ordinances of God. The root word in ordinances is order. In the Book of Joshua, we see God commanding the sun and moon to stand still and aid the people of God in battle. (Joshua 10:12). It was in the wondering years of the Israelites that God would guide them by a pillar of fire by night. (Exodus 13:21). This lets us know that God is the ruler of the affairs of man in the day and in the night season of our lives, that no matter how dark the night, He yet guides us as our light. This is the purpose of darkness: to show the glory of God (Psalm 8:3; 1 Cor.15:41).

"Jesus answered them, have not I chosen you twelve, and one of you is a devil?" (St. John 6:70)

Judas Iscariot, widely known as the *"son of perdition,"* was chosen as one of the 12 original disciples of Jesus. Judas followed Jesus throughout His earthly ministry. He held a very vital position in Jesus' administration as treasurer. He was in the midst of light, but yet he walked in darkness. Since true light can always detect darkness, Jesus knew who He was and what He was all about. Jesus never exposed the darkness because it had a purpose.

Jesus was the fulfillment of the prophecy of the seed of the woman that would bruise the head of the serpent (Genesis 3:15). He came into the world to be the sacrificial lamb without blemishes or stains to die for the sin of the world.

For 42 generations, the prophets foretold of His coming. They spoke of His death. How He would die and hang on a tree (Deuteronomy 21:23). They would laugh at him scornfully (Psalm 22:7-8). How He would be pierced in the side (Zechariah 12:10). No bones would be broken (Numbers 9:12). They spoke of Jesus being struck in the face (Isaiah 52:14). All of these things were the will of God for the life of Jesus. *"For it pleased the Father that He would suffer"* (Isaiah 53:10).

All of these things were accomplished by evil men. The prophet Zechariah said that Jesus would be betrayed by a close a friend for 30 pieces of silver. This was fulfilled by Judas, the son of perdition (Zechariah 11:12-13; St. Matthew 26:14-16). All these evil men were deceived by the spirit of deception. They were workers of the darkness. But it was done so that the scripture might be fulfilled.

Throughout the pages of the Scripture, we see evil men had a purpose in the overall plan of God. Those who work in darkness and are not children of the light are often instruments to the growth and the advancement of the people of God. It was Pharaoh that was set over the children of Israel. A hard taskmaster to afflict them with heavy burdens. The Egyptians made them serve rigorously. With bitterness, they made them serve. But the more they afflicted them, the more they multiplied and grew (Exodus 1:12) because true light always shines brighter in darkness.

It was under the tutelage of Eli, the Priest who had failed to walk in the ordinance of God and allowed the corruption of his sons in the

Temple, the lamp of God became dim, signifying spiritual blindness. Yet God places Samuel the Prophet to be trained and become the light of that time. It was in this dark era that the first open vision was given (1 Samuel 3:1-21).

Even more, King Saul, who was rejected by God and tormented by an evil spirit, plotted to kill David, whom God had chosen as his replacement. Under his shadow, David emerged as a man after God's Heart (Acts 13:22). Through this, we see that since the events of creation, light has always come out of darkness.

The Wheat and the Tare

The parable of the wheat and the tare is a final point to draw on. Jesus said it is like unto the Kingdom of Heaven. In our walk with God, we will often encounter those who have infiltrated our ranks and landed on our shores but are not one of us. These are those who have crept in unawares and do not have our common salvation (Jude 1:3-4). They fly high, taking pleasure in their ungodly ways. They are among us, but they are not of us. They are the Ananiases, Sapphiras, and Judas Iscariots. They are the Abner that make themselves strong for the house of Saul (2 Samuel 3:6).

They have been strategically planted by satan to weaken the plan of God and to cause the Word of God to have no effect. The enemy has deceived these people to make them think they are undetected. The Book of Jude speaks of these that have gone in the way of Cain, greed after the error of Balaam, but they perish in the gainsaying of Core (Jude 1:11). Their hearts are darkened (Ephesians 4:18), and their conscience is sealed (1 Timothy 4:2). The discerning heart knows them because the Word of God is inside us. The Word of God is a discerner of the thoughts and intents of the heart (Hebrews 4:12), but how do we deal with what we know, see, and perceive?

> *The Bible says that we are required to know the spirit of error and the spirit of truth. To try the spirit to see if it is of God. For He would that we be not ignorant and we are admonished to abound in wisdom and knowledge, but wisdom brings grief, and knowledge increases sorrow. (Ecclesiastes 1:18)*

Therefore, Jesus gives us the answer in the parable of the wheat and the tare. The farmer sowed good seed in his field, but while he slept, his enemy came and sowed tares among the wheat, and the Bible says he went his way. The enemy left the scene of the crime and thought he was undetected. He thought that his evil deed would ruin the crop. He failed to realize that *"No weapon that is formed against thee shall prosper; and every tongue that shall rise against thee in judgment thou shalt condemn. This is the heritage of the servants of the LORD, and their righteousness is of me, saith the Lord"* (Isaiah 54:17).

The enemy failed to realize that out of the dust, we rise to fulfill God's ultimate plan for our lives. *"If God is for us, who can be against us?"* (Romans 8:31). When the crop began to produce, the owner of the field said to the farmer that there was tare in the midst of the wheat. They were able to differentiate because the wheat brought fruits, and the tare did not.

They had grown together, and no one was the wiser because they were similar in the maturing phases. They were both able to stand in the elements of the weather and to stand the pruning of the farmer. They were allowed to grow together because the tare has many benefits for a healthier garden.

Weeds in the garden cause the lawn to grow thicker. Weeds thrive in an imbalanced soil condition and help bring the soil back in balance, and one of the most beneficial is that weeds provide food for microbes and insects. The owner knew that the tare had a divine purpose. However, he would separate the two at the time of the harvest. In a private conversation away from the multitude, Jesus explains this parable to His followers. The Sower is the Son of Man. The field is the world, and the good seeds are the sons of the Kingdom of God. The tare are the sons of the wicked one, the enemy who sowed the tare is the devil, The harvest is the end of the world, and the reapers are the angels (St. Matthew 13:24-30).

In the story, we see that the enemy has planted evil men(tare) in the world, and they are allowed to grow and flourish. The spirit of deception has deceived them to make them think that the harvest will never come and they will never be identified. *"For the wicked will soon be cut down"* (Psalm 37:2). But *"The meek shall inherit the earth and live in peace"* (Psalm 37:11). The Word of the Lord makes it very clear that these evil men will be gathered at the end of the world and burned in eternal fire.

Conclusion

"But thanks be unto God who gives us the victory through Jesus Christ." (1 Corinthians 15:57)

You and I do not have to be prey to the spirit of deception. We can live in the truth of the written Word of God. You and I do not have to be a part of the kingdom of darkness. We can walk as children of the light. You and I do not have to be ignorant of the enemy's devices. We can be full of the knowledge of God. You and I can be a light that shines in a dark world. And yes, we can know the spirit of error and the spirit of truth.

Made in the USA
Columbia, SC
28 May 2025

58517494R00052